RUMI AND CONFUCIUS

RUMI AND CONFUCIUS
Messages for a New Century

İbrahim Özdemir

New Jersey

Copyright © 2013 by Tughra Books

16 15 14 13   1 2 3 4

All rights reserved. No part of this book may be reproduced or transmitted in any form or by any means, electronic or mechanical, including photocopying, recording or by any information storage and retrieval system without permission in writing from the Publisher.

Published by Tughra Books
345 Clifton Ave., Clifton,
NJ, 07011, USA

www.tughrabooks.com

Library of Congress Cataloging-in-Publication Data Available

ISBN: 978-1-59784-272-3

Printed by
Çağlayan A.Ş., Izmir - Turkey

CONTENTS

Preface vii
A Quotation ix

I. INTRODUCTION 1

II. CONFUCIUS 13
   Life 15
   Teachings 21
      Cosmos and Nature 21
      Confucian Values 26
   Family 33
   Music 35

III. RUMI 37
   Life 39
   His Works 45
   Teachings 47
      God and Creation 47
   Nature as Mirror 53
      Rumi Conversing with a Sea-Monster 53
      Love as a Dynamic Force 55
      Animals as Brothers and Sisters 58
   Humanity 61
   Family 63
   Music 67

IV. CONCLUSION 71

References 77

Appendix I: Selected Quotations of Confucius 81

Appendix II: Selected Quotations of Rumi 85

About the Author..91

PREFACE

The first draft of this work was originally presented to the Second International Conference of The Asian Philosophical Association, held on October 26–29, 2006, in Pusan, S. Korea. The theme of conference was "The Rise of Asian Community and the New Dialogue between Past and Future of the World". To gain a better understanding of some major problems of our time, an examination of two great thinkers, Confucius and Rumi, is very crucial. I hope this book contributes to the spirit of the conference and initiates a dialogue between Confucian and Islamic civilizations.

Arnold Toynbee, the famous British historian, once said "… to solve the social problem of 21st century, we have to rely on the teachings of Confucius" and other great personalities of the past. Therefore, it is meaningful and timely to study some core ideas of Confucius and Rumi.

I want to thank Professor Alparslan Açıkgenç and Professor Choi Woo-Won, the co-organizers of the conference. They encouraged me to present the first draft of this work. More importantly, they provided a platform for philosophers from East and West to meet each other and engage in a meaningful dialogue.

I also want to thank Ahmet Çalışır, the Director and Conductor of the Konya Mystical Musical Group. We had a very enlightening talk during our visit to some historical places in Pusan. Mr. Çalışır is a Sufi musician, singer and performer, a man of heart and spirituality. He encouraged me to develop my paper into this book.

I would like to express my deepest gratitude to Fatma Açıkgenç and Hasan Horkuç for their careful reading of the first draft of this work.

I developed the original paper and used a more readable style to make it accessible to the general reader. Therefore, I removed all footnotes from the text. However, I listed all relevant references at the end.

We hope that this humble work provides a bridge between Rumi's teachings and Confucian wisdom, a bridge between the heart of Islam and Eastern wisdom.

A QUOTATION

Through international cooperation, efforts will need to be intensified to portray and instill a positive meaning of tolerance as a bedrock for a culture of peace, in the fight against racism and discriminations of all sorts, and to help prevent the outbreak of conflicts in various fields.

UNESCO continues to be committed to the promotion of a culture of peace in various ways and through all its major programmes.

Relevant activities include the dialogue among civilizations, cultures and peoples aimed at re-defining the logic, purpose and modalities of such dialogue, the promotion of quality education, reform of curricula and revision of school textbooks and materials.

In the context of the dialogue among civilizations, cultures and peoples broader adherence to religions and beliefs will introduce new dimensions, to which UNESCO will have to respond.

Source: Discussion paper prepared by the Director-General of UNESCO for the global consultation on the long-term future role of UNESCO

I.

Introduction

The sun rises every morning from the east. We look to the east to witness the beginning of a new day. The light of the sun not only fills our home and the world, but also gives us hope to begin a new day.

For centuries, generations have also looked to the East for the wisdom it contains and presents to us. This is not nostalgia for the past. On the contrary, it is a humble attempt to learn from the ancient wisdom of humanity, to open up our mind and spirit to the light rising from the East.

In this spirit, this humble work tries to compare and contrast the anthropocosmic insights of two great thinkers, Confucius (551–479 BCE) and Rumi (1209–1271), on nature, family, and music. By doing this, I hope to raise an environmental awareness, as well as a dialogue of civilizations. In fact, we return to the teachings of great thinkers and leaders of humanity, such as Confucius, Socrates, Buddha, Jesus, peace be upon him, Muhammad, peace and blessings be upon him, Rumi, Gandhi and others, again and again. We do so because they contain some essential truth, wisdom, and lessons that infuse our mundane activities with meaning.

The German philosopher Karl Jaspers (1883–1969) coined the idea of Axial Age to describe the coincident appearance of several major world religious and philosophical founders between 800 to 200 BCE. Jaspers argues that, "in this age were born the fundamental categories within which we still think today". Therefore, this age was regarded as a breaking point in ancient civilizations of the East and West. Confucius and Socrates, for example, "challenged the contemporary belief by their way of radical questioning; the Hebrew Prophets and Zoroaster both defended monotheism against the prevailing polytheism; Upanishads ended the pantheistic Vedas by emphasizing that Brahman and Atman are one; and Buddha sought to reform Hinduism by founding the new sect of Buddhism". In a nutshell, these great thinkers were concerned with human's potentialities and his existential situation by trying to respond to a set of ultimate questions:

Who am I?

Where do I come from?

Where am I going?

What is the meaning of nature?

What is the meaning of cosmos?

These are the ultimate questions that nobody can escape. We can postpone them, but cannot break away from them. The gravity of these questions can be seen in the life of great personalities. Socrates, for example, stated that "the unexamined life is not worth living". In this context, we should remember the famous Russian writer Leo Tolstoy, who asked himself this inevitable question at the zenith of his career: "What is the meaning of my life?" He then devoted the next thirty years of his life searching for a coherent answer to his question.

The prophets, mystics, philosophers, and poets of the Axial Age proposed their answers to these questions, too. Karen Armstrong, for example, in her new book, *The Great Transformation,* tries to understand the basic message and lessons we can learn from these personalities. Interestingly, she discovers that all Axial Age traditions emphasized justice and were committed to the practice of "disciplined sympathy" and "compassion". She also reminds us that "we have been living in a time of great social transformation and unrest, and, like the *axial sages*, we should foster compassion, self-emptying and justice". Needless to say, we can find and discover "a galaxy of spiritual stars in the Axial Age".

In this spirit, Rumi, a Sufi master of 13th century, can be added to the list of these great masters of life because he also devoted his life and energy responding to these questions. Moreover, there are striking spiritual, philosophical, and social similarities between Confucius and Rumi. They share more in common than most people think, and their teachings are still meaningful and relevant for today. They are resources of humanity that provide us a better and broader understanding of some major problems of the 21st century. Arnold Toynbee, the famous British historian, once declared that, "… to solve the social problem of the 21st century, we have to rely on the teachings of Confucius" and other great personalities of the past.

The global character of environmental problems, poverty, broken families, violence, and related issues also encourages us to see our problems in a different and wider context. Moreover, this global character has the potentiality of paving the way for a dialogue between East and West, sacred and secular. Dr. Anwar Ibrahim, former Deputy Prime Minster of Malaysia, said that "dialogue among civilizations is a global imperative. We live in one global and interconnected village. All living civilizations are crammed into this village, so we cannot be indifferent to one another. Nor can we talk down to one another. We must talk to one another and we must talk as equals." In the context of religion, Karen Armstrong calls the same phenomenon the "imperative to learn". She states, "We've got to know more about each other's religions so we don't harbor distorted, inaccurate images."

Another reason for this study is the far-reaching influence of Confucius' and Rumi's teachings on the next generations. "The Confucian tradition has a long historical legacy in East Asia extending from China across Korea and Japan and into Vietnam. [It] has influenced the Chinese attitude toward life, set the patterns of living and standards of social value, and provided the background for Chinese political theories and institutions". Moreover, the influence of Confucianism has been significant in political thought and institutions, social relationships and ritual exchange, educational philosophy and moral teaching, cultural attitudes, and historical interpretation.

Rumi lived in the western part of Asia, where East meets West, and the lands of Rumi became a bridge between Asia and Europe. Moreover, Rumi's philosophy and ideas have made a profound impact on the perception of Turks, Arabs, and Persians regarding the human-nature relationship over centuries. To the extent members of different faiths and religions coexisted and lived in peace in Turkey, it is due to Rumi's legacy.

And today, Rumi is widely considered by Western scholars to be the greatest mystical poet of all time. *Publishers Weekly* magazine named him the best-selling poet in America. Amazon.com lists more than

6,000 Rumi titles in books, tapes, CD's, and videos, (by everyone from Persian musicians and American scholars to New Age gurus like Deepak Chopra.) Even Madonna has recorded one of his poems.

What is more important to the present discussion, however, is the search of "the contemporary Anglo-American philosophical circles". They are also looking "in the direction of non-positivistic and dialectical discourse that underpins the very basic questions surrounding the meaning of life, history, and human existence". Therefore, it is not difficult to understand the recent intensive interest in the teachings of Confucius and Rumi.

It is evident that after a period of over 800 years after his birth, during which his fame has endured in the Middle East, Central Asia, and the Indian subcontinent, Rumi is still relevant. As an indication of relevance of his teachings for humanity, UNESCO designated the year 2007 in honor of his 800th birthday. (Studies also show that his ideas are still relevant and have a positive potential contribution for the East and West.)

UNESCO explained why it was honoring Rumi, "Eminent philosopher and mystical poet of Islam, Rumi advocated tolerance, reason and access to knowledge through love. His mystical relationship to Islam produced masterpieces that well beyond the borders of Turkey have marked Islamic culture and devotion. His work and thought continue to have universal relevance today."

It can rightly be asked, "Why is he, a man who lived and died in a culture so far removed from ours [the West] in time and temperament, so well-known and loved?" Shahram Shiva, a Persian who translates and performs Rumi's poems, answers this question as follows:

"He is accessible. He is almost eager to reach out to people, to touch people, to help them, to uplift them. This is not just a case of beautiful words on paper. It is a case of the cosmic force of this man who lived 800 years ago now living in this world in some subtle form, just as a saint or a Prophet would."

According to Soudabeh Sadigh, "The popularity of this great poet is rooted in the world's quest for spirituality as Rumi's poems reflect human's quest for love". Karen Armstrong explains further, "Rumi's spirituality is suffused by a sense of cosmic homelessness and separation from God, the Divine source."

The teachings of Confucius have been compared and contrasted with many philosophers and religious leaders. For example, Tang Junyi (1909–1978) of Hong Kong contrasted "Confucian self-cultivation with Greek, Christian, and Buddhist spiritual exercises. He concludes that Confucianism's commitment to the world, combined with its profound reverence for Heaven, offered a unique contribution to human[kind] flourishing in the modern world."

This work will limit itself to Confucian anthropocosmic cosmology and Rumi's perception of nature and human beings. It will also summarize their views on family and music to support the first proposition. We hope that this will enrich and broaden our perception of the natural world and our relationship with it. In Confucian terminology, we hope it may re-educate us regarding one of major challenges of modern world. If we neglect and cannot respond to this challenge with a creative and holistic method, it may lead us to a total collapse of modern civilization as convincingly argued by Diamond in his last book *Collapse: How Societies Choose to Fail or Succeed*.

One of the striking similarities of these "paradigmatic individuals" can be easily understood from their biographies. Confucius and Rumi were born into a time of "social upheaval and political turmoil". In the poetic expression of W.B. Yeats, it was a world in which "things fall apart; the center cannot hold. Mere anarchy is loosed upon the world." Therefore, both thinkers tried to provide means for their followers to overcome their difficult times, first by understanding, cultivating, and realizing their human potentialities, and then by transforming themselves, their families, and societies as well.

Most importantly, Rumi himself invites the world to join him in his spiritual journey of searching for a meaningful life:

> Come, come, whoever you are.
> Wanderer, idolater, worshipper of fire,
> Come even though you have broken your
> vows a thousand times,
> Come, and come yet again,
> Ours is not a caravan of despair.

II.

Confucius

LIFE

Confucius was born in the state of Lu, somewhere near the present town of Qufu in southeastern Shandong. His real name was K'ung Fu-tzu, which means "the Master" (K'ung). The Latin form, Confucius, is derived from K'ung Fu-tzu.

Confucius was a relatively ordinary person. His family was from the lesser aristocracy and had fallen on extremely hard times when he was born. He became an orphan at an early age and his older brother was a cripple. Therefore, as a young man Confucius had to care for his family's livestock and also had undertaken accounting for a while. He seems to have never attended school and was largely self-educated, eventually becoming China's most famous teacher, philosopher, and political theorist.

One day he said regarding poverty:

"It is better to be poor and yet happy; rich and yet fond of your fellowmen;" and, "To eat vegetables and drink only water, with bent arms for a pillow, I am still happy in such a life."

Just like other great personalities of the Axis Age, he was born into a time of social upheaval and political turmoil in China. As a result, he had to leave his state and go into exile. In fact, not only in early Chinese tradition, in other ancient cultures as well, exile and suffering were common themes in the lives of great personalities and heroes. Confucius was not an exception.

Confucius left Lu and traveled in the states of Wei, Song, Chen, Cai, and Chu. His students accompanied him. He was looking for a ruler who might employ him. Instead of sympathy and support from rulers, he found indifference, severe hardship, and danger.

Disappointed with the behavior of the ruling class, Confucius returned to Lu in 484 BCE and spent the remainder of his life, teaching students and working on some of his most famous works. Through teaching the youth, he hoped that he could change the world by changing its future leaders.

Like Socrates, Confucius left no books. However, his teachings were compiled by his devoted students and preserved in the *Analects*. *As Socrates was regarded as the father of philosophy and wisdom in the West, Confucius was the father of philosophy, wisdom, and wit in the East. We can see the huge impact of his teachings in the East and South East Asia.*

Confucius had a passion for music. One day, when he was thirty-six years old, he heard the music of The Succession Dance commemorating the inauguration of the legendary Emperor Shun. The music permeated his psyche and he became speechless. Later he exclaimed, "I did not imagine that any music existed which could reach such perfection as this."

Confucius' major emphasis, however, was on education and study. Study, for Confucius, meant finding a good teacher and imitating his words and deeds. He was willing to teach "anyone, whatever their social standing, as long as they are eager and tireless. He taught his students morality, proper speech, government, and the refined arts".

He also emphasized the importance of mastering the "Six Arts": ritual, music, archery, chariot riding, calligraphy, and computation. Morality, however, was the most important and dear subject for him.

He was a thinker, political figure, educator, and founder of the *Ru* School of Chinese thought. In spite of his practical abilities and his reputation for wisdom, Confucius had difficulty finding a suitable position in government. He was willing to do any type of work as long as it was ethical, but if honest work was not available, he was happy continuing his studies. "If any means of escaping poverty presented itself, which did not involve doing wrong, I would adopt it, even though employment was that of the gentleman who holds the whip. But as long as it is a question of illegitimate means, I shall continue to pursue the quests that I love."

Confucius' humility and industriousness set a good example and gave him a deeper understanding of common people. He occupied himself with learning from a very early age: "At fifteen my mind was set on learning. At thirty my character had been formed. At forty, I had no more perplexities. At fifty I knew the Will of Heaven. At sixty I was at ease with whatever I heard. At seventy I could follow my heart's desire without transgressing moral principles."

Confucius is the first professional teacher that we know of in ancient China. Although he was unsuccessful as a politician, there was no doubt that he was one of the world's greatest teachers. In Huston Smith's words, "he was [a] one-man university" just like Socrates. More interesting, his method of teaching was also that of Socrates. Like Socrates who taught a wide range of topics, Confucius instructed in "history, poetry, government, propriety, mathematics, music, divination, and sports".

He strove diligently to learn, and the ancient teachings had a peculiar fascination for him: "I am not one who was born with knowledge. I love the ancient teachings and earnestly seek them."

Smith argues that, "power and wealth could have been his for the asking if he had been willing to compromise with those in authority". However, he preferred his integrity and never regretted the choice:

"With coarse rice to eat, with water to drink, and my bended arm for a pillow—I have still joy in the midst of these things. Riches and honors acquired by unrighteousness are to me as a floating cloud."

As mentioned above, Confucius' discussions with disciples were compiled posthumously in *the Analects*, which contain an overview of his teachings. It can easily be seen from this work that Confucius presents himself as hungry human for learning, instead of a great scholar. He does not try to build a systematic theory of life and society, like Plato or Aristotle. He instructs his disciples "to think deeply for themselves and relentlessly study the outside world". Having a great respect for their master's learning, his students wanted to know how their master did his own studies. To this Confucius responded:

"I used to sit alone thinking about this and that. Sometimes I even forgot my meals or bedtime. Still I gained very little. Later I shifted to reading omnivorously, but I did not benefit a great deal either. At long last I came to see that reading in a mechanical way without using my brains was no use. On the other hand, if thinking is divorced from the reality and no due attention is paid to reading, one will continue to feel puzzled by many things. One should constantly review what he has learned and combine reading with thinking. Thus by making use of the theories one has learned to guide his thought and help analyze the problems at hand, progress will be achieved. "

He spent his last five years quietly teaching the classics. When he died in 479 BC, he was seventy-three years old. His death was deeply mourned by his students and some of them stayed by the side of his grave for as long as three years.

The Analects had been a fountain of inspiration and guidance for East Asian communities for thousands of years. In fact, any person who does not study the teachings and works of the Great Master was not considered morally upright or enlightened.

As his fame spread all over China and influenced the whole East and South East Asia, he has been regarded as "the mentor and model of ten thousand generations." Huston Smith, an American religious scholar born in China to missionaries and raised there, informs us that "for the past thousand years every Chinese school child until recently has raised his clasped hands each morning to a tablet in the corner bearing Confucius' name."

Virtually every Chinese student has poured over his sayings for hours with the result that these have become a part of the "Chinese mind." Moreover, remembering his influence on Chinese government, Confucianism regarded as "the greatest single intellectual force" in history.

TEACHINGS

Cosmos and Nature

For Confucius, nature is an important source. To understand the Confucian concept of nature we should look at it from a holistic and comprehensive perspective:

"The heaven appearing before us is only this bright, shining spot; but when taken in its immeasurable extent, the sun, moon, stars, and constellations are suspended in it, and all things are embraced under it. The earth, appearing before us, is but a handful of soil; but taken in all its breadth and depth, it sustains mighty Himalayas without feeling their weight; rivers and seas dash against it without causing it to leak. The mountain appearing before us is only a mass of rock; but taken in all the vastness of its size, grass and vegetation grow upon it, birds and beasts dwell on it, and treasures of precious stones are found in it. The water appearing before us is but a ladleful of liquid; but taken in all its unfathomable depths, the largest crustaceans, fishes, and reptiles are produced in them, and all useful products abound in them."

The first behavior Confucius expects from an attentive "virtuous man" has three aspects:

- Awe for Heaven's decree,
- Awe for great men, and
- Awe for saints' words

As we see, the fundamental attitude of human toward nature is awe. Confucius said, "There is nothing more visible than what is secret, and nothing more manifest than what is minute. Therefore the superior man is watchful over himself, when he is alone." It is our obligation to watch the natural order carefully and discover "the moral order of the universe", where everything is alive, active, and meaningful. As it will echo in the Sufi vision of Rumi below, there is a moral order in the universe which includes humans. According to the Confucian worldview, "the moral order of the macrocosm has to be enquired into; with veneration it should be studied; man must find out how he is the exact copy of that macrocosm and how the same moral order governs both. Ethics more than metaphysics, moral worth more than intellectual acquisition, are the means recommended."

Nature is like a meaningful book, full of wisdom. We have to learn and understand this book. Only then we can develop a meaningful and moral life, which is an exemplification of the "universal moral order." Chung Yung states

> The life of the vulgar person is a contradiction of that order.... To find the central clue to our moral being which unites us to the universal order, that indeed is the highest human attainment....
>
> The wise mistake moral law for something higher than what it really is; and the foolish do not know enough what moral law really is....
>
> The noble natures want to live too high, high above their moral ordinary self; and the ignoble do not live up to their moral ordinary self.
>
> There is no one who does not eat and drink. But few there are who really know the taste of what they eat and drink.

We should keep in mind that the central idea is that "the individual is regarded as the builder of the state and the empire through the family; he builds by discarding privileges and assuming responsibilities; he achieves this by practicing filial piety and thus moves from the condition of inferiority to that of morality; and then by practicing Jen ultimately reaches Divinity."

One should not neglect his obligation to his parents, and then extend this courtesy to nature because we are a part of creation.

Tu Weiming, a Harvard historian who has focused his career on the study of Confucianism and on revitalizing Confucianism for the twenty-first century, is the first scholar who "extends his interpretation of Confucianism to include ecological issues and beyond". He argues that the Confucian teachings can be understood in a way that it provides us moral grounds for environmental ethics. He begins with a reference to the following passage from *The Great Learning*:

"The ancients who wished clearly to exemplify illustrious virtue throughout the world would first set up good government in their states. Wishing to govern their states well, they would first regulate their families. Wishing to regulate their families, they would first cultivate their persons. Wishing to cultivate their persons, they would first rectify their minds. Wishing to rectify their minds, they would first seek sincerity in their thoughts. Wishing for sincerity in their thoughts, they would first extend their knowledge. The extension of knowledge lay in the investigation of things. For only when things are investigated is knowledge extended; only when knowledge is extended are thoughts sincere and so on back through the litany to peace in the world."

As we see, our responsibilities include the natural world and beyond. In other words, "we are responsible not only to self, family, community, state, and world, but also to the entire cosmos". Weiming argues that this understanding has great underpinnings for ecological awareness. However, he recognizes the "wholesale ecological disaster within Asia." Weiming argues that this apparent degradation and disaster in not necessarily stemming from Confucian values. Rather, it is the result of "a Europe centered mentality—the desire for 'development'—may have led to these problems, and certainly provides no solution."

It is true that the modern scientific worldview is a Western phenomenon and its influence can be felt everywhere; East Asia and Islamic lands are not an exception to this. S. H. Nasr makes a similar observation regarding the huge environmental degradation in the Muslim world, concluding that the "Islamic world is not totally Islamic today, and much that is Islamic lies hidden behind the cover of Western cultural, scientific, and technological ideas and practices emulated and aped to various degrees of perfection, or rather one should say of imperfection, by Muslims during the past century".

Weiming, in this context, encourages Asia to look "beyond Europe to symbolic resources based on its own ancient traditions" for a more holistic and sustainable developmental model. In this spirit, we can study the core teachings of Confucius and Rumi and their relevance for environmental awareness and ethics in some detail.

Confucian Values

The key concepts of Confucian ethics can be summarized as Jen, variously translated as love, goodness, humanity, righteousness, propriety, integrity, and filial piety. In other words,

- To love others;
- To honor one's parents;
- To do what is right instead of what is of advantage;
- To practice "reciprocity", in other words, "don't do to others what you would not want done to yourself"; and
- To rule by moral example, instead of by force and violence (Analects XII: 19).

These key elements, which have endured despite historical changes and political upheavals, articulate a new worldview:

- A dynamic cosmological context or worldview for promoting harmony amidst change;
- The embeddedness of each person in concentric circles of relationships and ethical responsibilities;
- The importance of the family including past, present, and future generations;

- The function of a hierarchical social system where loyalties to elders and to teachers are critical;
- The significance of education in cultivating the individual, enriching the society, and contributing to the political order;
- The role of government in establishing a political bureaucracy for ruling large numbers of people; and
- The value of history as an element of civilizational continuity and moral rectification.

In contrast to the modern scientific worldview, Confucian values "promote harmony amidst change". For many ecologists, only this perception of reality provides us with "an invaluable perspective for seeing nature as intrinsically valuable and for understanding the role of the human in relation to natural processes as critical". When we examine this worldview we see that it is characterized by "four key elements":

- An anthropocosmic rather than an anthropocentric perspective;
- An organic holism of the continuity of being;
- A dynamic vitalism of material force *(ch'i, qi)*; and
- A comprehensive ethics embracing both humans and nature.

Professor Tucker clarifies the meaning of these key elements. "By "anthropocosmic", she explains, "we refer to the great triad of heaven (a guiding force), earth (nature), and humans. This idea is central to Confucian thought from its earliest expressions in the classical texts to its later developments in Neo-Confucianism which arose in the eleventh century."

By "organic holism", she states, "the universe is seen as unified, interconnected, and interpenetrating. Everything interacts and affects everything else, which is why the notion of microcosm and macrocosm is so essential to Chinese cosmology. The elaboration of the interconnectedness of reality can be seen in the correspondence of the five elements with seasons, directions, colors, and even virtues. This type of classification began in the third millennium BCE and resulted in texts such as the *I Ching (Book of Changes)*. This sense of holism is characterized by the view that there is no Creator God behind the universe. Chinese thought is less concerned with theories of origin or with concepts of a personal God than with the perception of an ongoing reality of a self-generating, interconnected universe described by Tu Weiming as a "continuity of being."

"Dynamic vitalism", according to Tucker, "refers to the basis of the underlying unity of reality which is constituted of *ch'i*, the material force of the universe. This is the unifying element of the cosmos and creates the basis for a profound reciprocity between humans and the natural world. Material force *(ch'i)* as the substance of life is the basis for the continuing process of change and transformation in the universe. The term *sheng-sheng,* namely, "production and reproduction" is repeatedly used in Confucian texts to illustrate the creativity of nature".

Tucker continues, "This recognition of the ceaseless movement of the cosmos arises from a profound meditation on the fecundity of nature in continually giving birth to new life". Furthermore, "it constitutes a sophisticated awareness that change is the basis of the interaction and continuation of the web of life systems—mineral, vegetable, animal, and human. Finally, it celebrates transformation as the clearest expression of the creative processes of life with which humans should harmonize their own actions". In essence, human beings are urged to "model themselves on the ceaseless vitality of the cosmic process."

According to Julian Huxley "nature is not a mechanism, but a process". Therefore, "to define human's place in nature, we must discover what situation he/she occupies in the process; to determine their role, we need to discover something of the essential characters not only of nature, but of man himself as a resultant within its process; and this exploration will lead to new views on the unity of knowledge."

Moreover, according to Huxley "dynamic vitalism" and this exploration will lead to new views on the unity of knowledge. As a result of this perception, the Cartesian dualism, which had dominated our modern perception of reality since the 17th century, disappears and humans become "biological-historical-ethical beings who live in a universe of complex correspondences and relationships." According to Professor Arthur Kane Scott, recent findings in science support this understanding: "The picture that Hubble portrays of the cosmos, along with the discoveries made in modern physics by Einstein, Heisenberg and Bohr reveal a universe dramatically different from the mechanistic-dualistic-reductionastic picture drawn by Newton, Descartes, and Bacon in the 17th century."

In other words, as A.N. Whitehead emphasizes, "nature is [not] a dull affair, soundless, scentless, colorless: merely the hurrying of material, endlessly, meaninglessly". We are not living amid "a senseless, meaningless world". A good example of how Confucian values transform us is the former Marxist thinker Feng Youlan (1895–1990) of Beijing, who rejected his previous commitment to the Marxist notion of struggle and stressed the value of harmony, not only in the human world, but also in the relationship between humans and nature." Youlan's return to the philosophy of harmony of Zhang Zai

(1020–1077) signaled a departure from his Marxist phase and a representation of his Confucian ideas in the 1940s, prior to the founding of the People's Republic of China. The opening lines in Zhang Zai's *Western Inscription* state: "Heaven is my father and Earth is my mother, and even such a small creature as I find an intimate place in their midst. Therefore that which fills the universe I regard as my body and that which directs the universe I consider as my nature. All people are my brothers and sisters, and all things are my companions".

According to Weiming, the *Western Inscription* can be regarded "as a core Neo-Confucian text" in articulating the anthropocosmic vision of the unity of Heaven, Earth, and Humanity. Accordingly, Feng characterizes the highest stage of human self-realization as the embodiment of the "spirit of Heaven and Earth". In Tucker's words, "human livelihood and culture was seen as continuous with nature". The following passage by a leading Han Confucian, Tung Ch'ung-shu (c. 179–c.104 BCE) states this very clearly:

> Heaven, earth, and humans are the basis of all creatures.
>
> Heaven gives them birth, earth nourishes them, and humans bring them to completion. Heaven provides them at birth with a sense of filial and brotherly love, earth nourishes them with cloth-

> ing and food, and humans complete them with rites and music.
>
> The three act together as hands and feet join to complete the body and none can be dispensed with.

Within this broad cosmological pattern of Confucian thought the person is seen in relationship to others and not as an isolated individual. Thus, there are more grounds in Confucianism for emphasizing the common good that is critical for developing environmental ethics. It seems that Western traditions tend to underscore the importance of the individual, focusing on individual rights and freedoms. The Confucian tradition, however, stresses the importance of cooperative group effort so that individual concerns are sublimated to a larger sense of the common good. In this view, self-interest and altruism for a common cause are not mutually exclusive, and responsibilities rather than rights are stressed. Such a communitarian value system may be indispensable for fostering sustainable communities.

FAMILY

With the Confucian emphasis on the continuity of the family there is a strong ethic of indebtedness to past generations and obligations to descendants. Within this moral framework there is the potential for evoking a sense of self-restraint and communal responsibility toward the environmental well-being of future generations. In other words, the Confucian emphasis on lineage (ensuring continuity from the ancestors to the heirs) may be raised to another ethical perspective, namely, "intergenerational obligations toward maintaining a healthy environment". On this basis it could be argued that unlimited development or unrestrained consumption must be curtailed.

The hierarchical social system of Confucianism can also be expanded to place humans in relation to the biological lineage of life in the natural world. In this sense, loyalty to elders, teachers, and those who have gone before, may be broadened to include respect for the complex ecosystems and forms of life that have preceded humans. Thus, biodiversity is valued. The total dependence of humans on other life-forms for survival and sustenance may be underscored in this scenario. "Loyalty" is enlarged from the human world to include the natural world itself.

In short, the Confucian worldview has "enormous potential for renewed appreciation of nature as intrinsically valuable but also as the source of personal vitality and moral integrity for sustaining the community of life. Moreover, this perspective values nature as the origin of all that sustains life itself from the basics of food, clothing, and shelter to innumerable sources of employment."

MUSIC

Confucius was also an outstanding musician. He could play numerous musical instruments and was good at composing and singing.

"When the master was in Ch'i, he heard the Shao, and for three months did not know the taste of flesh. "I did not think" he said, "that music could have been made so excellent as this."

Confucius told his son that if he did not study poetry, he would "have nothing to talk about," and if he did not study ritual, he would "have no way of taking [his] stand" (16:13, Analects).

"Learn ancient poetry and music. It will give you a broader perspective on things, give you more to talk about, and help you succeed in your family life and at work."

"When affairs cannot be carried on to success, proprieties and music do not flourish. When proprieties and music do not flourish, punishments will not be properly awarded. When punishments are not properly awarded, the people do not know how to move hand or foot."

III.

Rumi

LIFE

Jalal ad-Din Muhammad Rumi was born in 1207 in Balkh in what is today Afghanistan. The Muslim world honors him with the title of *Mawlana* (Our Master). He based his anthropocosmic worldview on the principle of love. It is this aspect of his deep vision of the universe and the place of humanity in it that attracts environmentalists and provides them with a new perspective to see the deeper dimension of reality.

When Rumi was twelve years old his family left Balkh in order to escape the Mongol invasion. The journey of family was westward and took four years. During this long journey, the young Rumi traveled extensively in Muslim lands, encountering majestic mountains and beautiful plains, visiting major cities, and meeting well-known Sufis and scholars of the time. His family performed the pilgrimage to Mecca and finally settled in Konya, Turkey, then part of the Seljuk Empire. He spent the rest of his life in Konya, which was a center of learning during Rumi's time. Moreover, Konya was "at the crossroad of the East and the West, only a short distance from Damascus—

one of the flourishing intellectual capitals of the world at the time".

From an early age Rumi studied religious sciences with his father, who was an eminent theologian, a great teacher, and preacher. Rumi also traveled to Aleppo and Damascus to study with some of the greatest religious minds.

We see in Rumi "a grand and illustrious life" as "a respected teacher, a master of Sufi lore, and the head of a university. At the age of thirty-four he claimed hundreds of disciples".

It seems that Rumi, just like Confucius, assimilated all traditional and conventional learning. He gradually perceived the limitation of ritual and realized that knowledge of ordinary life does not, in itself, bring rebirth in totality. An anecdote from *Fihi Ma Fihi* highlights this spiritual state and his attitude toward his students very eloquently:

"I have studied many sciences and taken pains to offer fine, rare and precious things to the scholars and researchers, the clever ones and the deep thinkers who come to me. God has willed this. He gathered to me all those sciences, and assembled here all those pains, so I would become occupied with this work. What can I do? In my own country, and amongst my own people, there is nothing more shameful than poetry. If I had remained there, I would have lived in harmony with their temperament. I would have practiced what they love, such as giving lectures, composing books and preaching."

Thus, he was not satisfied with theology and classical learning as he considered them to be occupied with formalism. Burhanu'l-Din Muhaqqiq of Tirmidh, one of his father's loyal students and a famous Sufi, visited Rumi and became his spiritual guide in Sufi teaching and practice. Rumi spent the next nine years with him. Eventually, Burhanu'l-Din, closely monitoring his disciple's intellectual development, told him that he was ready for a new mission:

> You are now ready, my son. You have no equal in any of the branches of learning. You have become a lion of knowledge. I am such a lion myself and we are not both needed here and that is why I want to go.
>
> Furthermore, a great friend will come to you, and you will be each other's mirror. He will lead you to the innermost parts of the spiritual world, just as you will lead him. Each of you will complete the other, and you will be the greatest friends in the entire world.

The great transformation in Rumi's life began in 1244, when the "enigmatic figure Shams ad-Din of Tabriz, the expected friend" arrived in Konya. Rumi was forty years old. He found in Shams "the perfect image of the Divine Beloved which he had long been seeking". For him, Shams was "the light of the eye, the clarity of reason, the brightness of the soul, and the enlightenment of the heart". He took Shams to his house, and for a year or two they remained inseparable. Rumi was re-born after meeting with Shams and then discovered love as the dynamic force of universe. Everything after Shams' arrival changed. In his majestic poetry, Rumi states:

> I was dead, I became alive;
> I was weeping, I became laughing; the power
> of love came, and I became everlasting power.
> My eye is satiated, my soul is bold, I have the
> heart of a lion, I have become shining Venus.

Rumi's son, Sultan Walad, vividly describes the "passionate and uncontrollable emotion which overwhelmed his father at this time":

> Never for a moment did he cease from listening to music (*sama*), and dancing;
> Never did he rest by day and night.
> He had been a mufti: he became a poet;
> He had been an ascetic: he became intoxicated by Love.
> 'T was not the wine of the grape: the illuminated soul drinks only the wine of Light.

According to William Chittick, a well-known scholar on Rumi and Sufism, "Shams seems to have opened Rumi up to certain dimensions of the mysteries of Divine love that he had not yet experienced". Their closeness led some of Rumi's disciples to become jealous, and eventually Shams disappeared. Some whispered that he had been murdered, but Rumi himself does not seem to have believed the rumors. What is clear is that Shams' disappearance was the catalyst for Rumi's extraordinary outpouring of poetry. Rumi makes this point explicit in many passages. He alludes to it in the first line of his great *Mathnawi*, where he states:

> Listen to this reed as it tells its tale,
> Complaining of separations.

When Rumi died on December 17, 1273, Jews, Christians, and Muslims alike attended his funeral. All regarded him as their master. The night he passed away was named "*Shab-e Arus*" (Wedding Night—symbolizing reunion with God). Ever since, the Mawlawi dervishes have kept that date as a festival.

Farewell of Rumi

The day I've died, my pall is moving on
But do not think my heart is still on earth!
Don't weep and pity me: "Oh woe, how awful!"
You fall in devil's snare—woe, that is awful!
Don't cry "Woe, parted!" at my burial
For me this is the time of joyful meeting!
Don't say "Farewell!" when I'm put in the grave
A curtain is it for eternal bliss.
You saw "descending"—now look at the rising!

Is setting dangerous for sun and moon?
To you it looks like setting, but it's rising;
The coffin seems a jail, yet it means freedom.
Which seed fell in the earth that did not grow there?
Why do you doubt the fate of human seed?
What bucket came not filled from out the cistern?
Why should the soul of Yusuf then fear this well?
Close here your mouth and open it on that side.
So that your hymns may sound in Where-no-place!

HIS WORKS

Rumi's major works include the *Mathnawi*, in six volumes with about 25,000 verses. It has been called the "Koran in Persian" by Jami, one of the greatest Sufi poets in the 15th century. His other major works are the *Diwan-e Shams-e Tabrizi*, which comprises some 40,000 verses, *Fihi Ma Fih* (In It What's in It), which has Rumi's speeches on different subjects, and *Majalis-i Sab'a* (seven sessions) which contains seven sermons given in seven different assemblies.

According to Reynold Alleyne Nicholson (1868–1945), who dedicated his life to studying Islam and Rumi, "While the *Mathnawi* is generally instructional in character, though it also has entertaining passages, as befits a book intended for the enlightenment of all sorts of students. The *Diwan*, however, and, on a much smaller scale, the *Rubayiat* are personal and emotional in appeal. Lyrics and quatrains alike have everywhere the authentic ring of spiritual inspiration, while in image, style and language they often approximate very closely to the *Mathnawi*."

Nicholson convincingly argues that, "in Rumi the Persian mystical genius found its supreme expression. Viewing the vast landscape of Sufi poetry, we see him standing out as a sublime mountain-peak; the other poets before and after him are but foot-hills in comparison. The influence of his example, his thought and his language is powerfully felt through all the succeeding centuries; every Sufi after him capable of reading has acknowledged his unchallenged leadership".

Arthur John Arberry (1905–1969), another expert and translator of Rumi, agrees with Nicholson, "In Rumi we encounter one of the world's greatest poets. In profundity of thought, inventiveness of image, and triumphant mastery of language, he stands out as the supreme genius of Islamic mysticism."

Eric Fromm adds, "Rumi was not only a poet and a mystic and the founder of a religious order; he was also a man of profound insight into the nature of man. He discussed the nature of the instincts, the power of reason over instincts, the nature of the self, of consciousness; the unconscious, and cosmic consciousness".

TEACHINGS

God and Creation

For Rumi, God, the Cosmic Ego, created the material world *ex nihilo*—out of nothing and never ceases to create new things. Everything has been created with a specific order, duty, purpose, and meaning. There is no lifeless matter in this system; all matter is alive, albeit at various gradations of being. According to Rumi, "earth, and water, fire and air are alive in the view of God, though they appear to be dead to us." He cautions us, "never think the earth void or dead; it is aware, it is awake and it is quivering."

Hegel, the great German philosopher, studied Rumi's teaching meticulously and admired his concept of *Unity of God*. In order to see *the consciousness of the One* in the world "… in its finest purity and sublimity", he recommends to consult Rumi, explaining,

> If, [for instance], in the excellent Jalaluddin Rumi in particular, we find the unity of the soul with the One set forth, and that unity

> described as love, this spiritual unity is an exaltation above the finite and vulgar, a transfiguration of the natural and the spiritual, in which the externalism and transitoriness [sic.] of immediate nature, and of empirical secular spirit, is discarded and absorbed.

Bina and Vaziri note that "Hegel is so impressed by Rumi's imagery and precision that he could not refrain from quoting long passages from his magnificent poetry".

This "supreme vision of reality" was peculiar to Sufism, which sees God everywhere, viewing every part of creation as a reflection of God's glory. The Sufi poet Jami of the 15th century writes, "Every branch and leaf and fruit reveals some aspect of God's perfection: the cypress gives hint of His majesty; the rose gives tidings of His beauty." Indeed, every atom was created by God so that man could know the highest truth and learn the secrets of love.

Theocentricism, therefore, is the key concept to understand Rumi's anthropocosmic worldview. God is goal of Rumi's thought. As Reza Arasteh observes, "*Mathnawi* first takes the novice in his present state and directs his entire attention toward an object of desire-generally the attributes of the guide or of God—or the creative force in the universe". His poetry thus is "nothing but an attempt to speak of God's grandeur as it reveals itself in the different aspects of life." For Rumi, God wants to be known, so manifests Himself out of His eternal qualities. Two of God's attributes are especially relevant in this regard: (1) God, the Nourisher of all realms and beings and (2) God who creates and sustains out of love. Furthermore, God is not a static Absolute, but a perpetually gushing fountain of eternal life manifesting His Majesty, Wisdom, and Knowledge through the universe.

Consequently, in the cosmic system as Rumi sees it, everything happens according to a great plan formulated by Divine Will and Wisdom. Even bees build their houses by inspiration from God. (So, a colorful and living world reveals itself in his poetry.) While everything is related and connected to each other, everything has also a special space, meaning, duty, and importance.

The cosmos, thus, becomes a meaningful book and a precious piece of art which manifest "the attributes and qualities" of its owner. Furthermore, the whole world—fish and moon, atom and sun—has been created to worship and love God, and to express its constant adoration in an intoxicated dance.

For Rumi, human beings are not outsiders and strangers in a hostile and brute natural environment. Rather, the whole world is a majestic garden, in which every flower has its function and represents various states and aspects of human life. Every leaf on a tree and every bird in a bush offer praise and gratitude for God's greatness and sustenance. Every leaf and tree is a messenger from non-existence, proclaiming the creative power of God, talking with long hands and green fresh tongues.

Rumi listens to the constant praise uttered by the flowers and all other creatures. He visualizes them in the various positions of prayer. A plane tree, for example, opens its hand in prayer just like a devoted Muslim does. The clouds are pregnant from the ocean of love: "as long as the clouds weep not, how the garden smiles."

The morning breeze is a fitting symbol for the life-giving breath of the Beloved that causes twigs and branches to become intoxicated and dance. Rumi reminds and teaches us that the morning breeze has secrets to tell and this is why we must not go back to sleep right after the Morning Prayer.

> The breeze at dawn has secrets to tell you.
> *Don't go back to sleep.*
> You must ask for what you really want.
> *Don't go back to sleep.*
> People are going back and forth
> across the doorsill where the two worlds touch.
> The door is round and open.
> *Don't go back to sleep.*

When Rumi looks at earth with this perception, he does not see it as "mere matter; lifeless and meaningless". Rather, earth appears to him as a Paradise.

And earth ever appears to me as a Paradise.
Each moment a flesh form, a new beauty,
So that weariness vanishes at these ever-fresh sights.
I see the world filled with blessings,
Fresh waters ever welling up from new fountains.
The sound of those waters reaches my ears,
My brain and senses are intoxicated therewith.
Branches of trees dancing like fair damsels,
Leaves clapping hands like singers.
These glories are a mirror shining through a veil;
If the mirror were unveiled, how would it be?
I tell not one in a thousand of them,
Because every ear is stopped with doubt.
To men of illusions these tales are mere good tidings,
But men of knowledge deem them not tidings, but ready cash.
Prayers to God to change our base inclinations and give us higher aspirations.

As we have observed, Rumi is "a passionate lover of all God's creation". We can see his deep love for nature: the manifestations of the Beautiful Names of God.

NATURE AS MIRROR

The whole of Rumi's poetry can be regarded as admiration of eternal Beauty as reflected in the cosmos. Therefore, he often uses a mirror as a symbol for the created world, which reflects the eternal Beauty of God. Since the natural world is a mirror of Divine beauty, God is closer to human beings than their jugular vein (Qaf 50:16). Rumi sees his Loving God's signs everywhere, and he never tires of repeating the marvels of God's creation—the result of the unceasing Divine Will and Power.

Now, we see Rumi in his majestic garden as listening, not only to the constant praise uttered by the flowers and all other creatures, but also visualizing them in various positions of prayer.

Rumi Conversing with a Sea-Monster

Indeed, the whole of Rumi's poetry can be regarded as admiration of eternal Beauty as reflected in the cosmos. It is the major human duty and responsibility "to recognize the real nature of every particle of the universe", because God created man in His own image. Then, everyone will see that even material world while from our perspective "they (the inanimate creatures) are dead"; from perspective of the Divine "they are living". When we look at reality with this Sufi vision, then we realize the whole reality with a new perspective. Rumi reminds us to study every particle of the universe with care, caution, and amazement, just like a lover of art who studies a masterpiece:

> When He sends them down to our world, the rod of Moses becomes a dragon in regard to us;
>
> The mountains sign with David, iron becomes as wax in his hand;
>
> The wind becomes a carrier for Solomon, the sea understands what God said to Moses concerning it.
>
> The moon obeys the sign given by Muhammad, the fire (of Nimrod) becomes a garden of roses for Abraham.
>
> They all cry, "We are hearing and seeing and responsive, though to you, the uninitiated, we are mute."

Instead of explaining nature by mechanical dynamics, he resorts to love as the fundamental urge that creates attraction and affinities: "All atoms in the cosmos are attracted to one another like lovers; everyone is drawn towards its mate by the magnetic pull of love."

The heavenly movements are waves in an infinite ocean of love. Without cosmic love all existence would freeze and shrink into nothingness. The organic would refuse to merge and emerge into vegetation; vegetation would not be lifted into animal life, nor would life ascend towards the mind and spirit. In short, without love, nothing would move.

Atoms are dancing!

O daylight, rise! Atoms are dancing,
Souls, lost in ecstasy, are dancing.
I'll whisper in your ear where the dance will take you.
All atoms in the air, in the desert,
They are all like madmen, each atom, happy or miserable,
Is Passionate for the sun of which nothing can be said.

Love as a Dynamic Force

For Rumi, a force—a secret energy—lies beneath the spiritual and material world, informing the invisible, progressive change in the universe (humanity included). This force is love, and it originates in God and moves towards God. According to Rumi, love is the positive energy that is responsible for the interaction between particles, thus connecting everything with everything else in the universe. Everything in the universe is interdependent and interconnected.

Everything's well-being is dependent on everything else.

Furthermore, Rumi reminds us that since love arouses every sense, increases the power of intuition, and leads to insight, love is superior to intellect in human life. In daily social life, for example, love has an important practical function: it solves disputes, eliminates selfishness and egotism, and draws aside all veils from the mind. Thus, love is not only basic and necessary for a religious and ethical life, but also for the sustainability of the cosmic order of the universe.

> My Mother is Love
> My Father is Love
> My Prophet is Love
> My God is Love
> I am a child of Love
> I have come only to speak of Love

In a nutshell, Rumi presents a deep and comprehensive understanding of the interdependence and interrelatedness of humanity and the natural world. In so doing, he affirms the reality of the world and dignity of all life, particularly of human life, which has become self-conscious and conscious of its Divine origin and goal.

Rumi passionately declares, "Love is the soul of the universe, and this soul knows no bounds—it embraces all people, all countries, and all religions".

If we look at the existentialist psychologist Eric Fromm's book *The Art of Loving*, we can find the full implications of this understanding. According to Fromm, "When we are 'in Love' the world seems sweeter, more beautiful, and more magnificent. When we fall in love, we are in love with everything and everyone".

However, Rumi asserts that merely to become aware of the power of love and relate oneself to others is not enough; "Man must translate his state of being, kindness, benevolence, and love into human conduct and creativity." It is obvious that Rumi is not satisfied with a mere intellectual transformation. Man "must" translate his belief and intellectual life in practice. "He must take a further step and discover the joy of being in active state of well-being in order to relate himself to his fellowmen" and [universe].

Therefore, Rumi goes beyond social institutions, such as the family, school, and other life experiences, and considers them "necessary only because of man's immaturity. All these should be directed toward the final rebirth of man and his attainment of 'the art of loving'". Interestingly, "This attitude of loving as well as man's insight into his human and non-human environment, stimulates man to create outwardly while experiencing happiness inwardly."

It is here where we can develop a whole environmental ethics, where humans can translate their inner peace and harmony toward the whole of creation. This attitude is not utilitarian and instrumental; it is a state of human condition as a humble member of cosmos.

Animals as Brothers and Sisters

According to Rumi, animals are not "machines or automata", as Cartesian philosophy would have us believe. Even the wolf, rooster, and lion know what love is. Therefore, Rumi was full of love and compassion toward all creatures of God, as many anecdotes from his work attest. For example, he would not drive a sleeping dog from his path, but rather would wait until the creature got up to leave..

One day Rumi was walking with his students on the streets of Konya. A cow approached and bowed to him with tears welling-up in her eyes. It was apparent that the poor animal was running away from something terrible. Rumi put his hand on animal's back and tried to calm her down. Two gentlemen then arrived with knives in their hands. Before they asked for the animal, Rumi told them what they wanted to do with the poor cow. They said that the cow belonged to them, and they wanted to slaughter it and sell the meat. After a short negotiation, Rumi convinced them not to kill this cow because it was too young. Everybody was speechless. Before they left, they promised that they would not slaughter the poor cow.

On another occasion, Rumi took a loaf of bread and left home. One of his disciples followed him secretly. He observed Rumi feeding a dog that had just given birth to a litter of seven. When Rumi realized that he had been followed, he explained to his student the situation with these words: "This poor dog gave birth a week ago. Although she was hungry for seven days, she never left her babies and took care of them with compassion. Our beloved Prophet Muhammad, peace and blessings be upon him, reminds us that: "The Most Merciful One is merciful towards those who are merciful. Act kindly to those on earth so that those in the heavens [the angels] will be merciful to you."

HUMANITY

Humanity is the central figure in God's creation, as well the vicegerent of God on earth. Being at the top of the great chain of being, even beyond it, makes humans more responsible toward the rest of creation. It is up to us to take care of the whole system. But we are not the owner of nature as such; the sole aim of nature is not to serve us and our ends.

The Sufi vision, on the other hand, teaches us that the whole creation is a gift from God and a sign of His creative power. Since God creates and sustains all ecosystems, human beings must interact with the natural world carefully and wisely. Moreover, we should use its natural resources with care, nurturing a relationship with it that is founded on love and compassion, which is the essence of all reality.

> Sometimes, even the angels envy our purity,
> And sometimes, even Satan sees us fearless and runs away.
> This soil is our soil which is charged with God's trust.
> May God preserve our power and nimbleness from evil.

In short, the natural world with its all majestic beauty and resources has been entrusted to us, as we are God's vicegerents on earth. We are not the lords of nature and the world; the world is not our property, at our disposal to be used haphazardly and irresponsibly. On the contrary, God created nature, and it belongs to Him.

As we see, spirituality, rationality, and universal morality have found a healthy synthesis in Rumi's thought: God, the universe, and humanity are embraced in a single all-encompassing vision, the vision of creative love.

FAMILY

Although we mentioned earlier that Rumi goes beyond social institutions, his concept of family has overreaching connotations as he sees the whole world as a family. In fact, his understanding of family is similar to the Confucian understanding. The only difference is the All-Knowing, All-Seeing, and All-Sustaining transcendental God of Rumi:

> We are the family of the Lord and His sucking babes.
> The Prophet said, "The people are God's family;"
> He who sends forth the rain from heaven,
> Can He not also provide us our daily bread?
> How all creatures cry to God for sustenance?

Needless to say, the world is our home. But the real owner is God. We are members among others. Cow, lion, wolf, ant, bee, in short all animals, are our brothers and sisters. We are the family of God, who is the Lord, Owner, and Sustainer of the planet earth. We all depend on His sustenance and care. Our role is that of stewardship toward the rest of family. Let's look at the world through Rumi's eyes:

> Yea, all the fish in the seas,
> And all feathered fowl in the air above,
> All elephants, wolves, and lions of the forest,
> All dragons and snakes, and even little ants,
> Yea, even air, water, earth, and fire,
> Draw their sustenance from Him, both winter and summer.
> Every moment this heave cries to Him, saying,
> "O Lord, quit not [Your] hold of me for a moment!
> The pillar of my being is [Your] aid and protection;
> The whole is folded up in that right hand of [Yours]."
> And earth cries, "O keep me fixed and steadfast,
> [You] who have placed me on the top of waters!"
> All of them are waiting and expecting His aid,
> All have learned of Him to represent their needs.

Here, we see the world as a home to all creatures inhabiting it. And the whole system, every day and every moment, is sustained by God. Besides the strong implications for sustainability of the system and the Sustainer, (the psychological dimension is amazing, giving us a sense of being at home.)

Moreover, we are not thrown or cast away to an alien and hostile world. We are not strangers amidst a hostile and crude environment. We are not alone, helpless and friendless. On the contrary, we are at home. Everything, animate and inanimate, has a spiritual bond with us. We are members of the same family. Our Creator, Owner, and Sustainer is the same God, who is nearer to us than our jugular vein.

As Rumi reminds us in his *Discourses*, God is always near to us: "Every thought and idea you conceive, there is God—for God gave being to that idea and thought. Yet God is so close you cannot see [Him]. What is so strange in that? In every act you perform, reason guides you and initiates your action, but you cannot see your reason. You see its effect, but you cannot see its essence."

In the same manner, we can see God everywhere and in everything, if only we look. He is beyond our physical sight and intellectual understanding, and at the same time, He is nearer to us than our jugular vein (Qaf 50:16). Rumi, as well as all Muslims, pray directly to God, with no intermediary. They seek guidance from Him alone, because God knows well the secrets of our hearts (al-Ma'idah 5:7).

> "When My servants ask you concerning Me,
> I am indeed close (to them).
> I respond to the prayer of every suppliant when he calls on Me.
> Let them also, with a will, Listen to My call, and believe in Me, that they may walk in the right way." (al-Baqarah 2:186)

In Rumi's understanding, the world is our home and nature is our mother. We are sucking babies. When sucking the breast of our mother, we should not bite and give her pain. Otherwise, she will push us away and she may even punish us. Ecological disasters and problems, therefore, can be seen as the result of mother earth's anger over our selfish and utilitarian mentality and attitudes toward her.

The implication for environmental awareness is self-evident: The world is our home and nature is our mother. Not only in Confucianism, but also in Islam we must respect our parents. We must respect our ancestors as well as our offspring.

In short, the skies with the sun, the moon and stars, and the face of the earth with flowers, trees, gardens, orchards, and the various animal species, adorn God and declare His greatness and majesty. He is the Sustainer of all systems who causes the rivers and streams to flow on the earth, who upholds the skies (without support), causes the rain to fall, and places the boundary between night and day. The universe with all its richness and vitality is the work and art of God, who unfolds and manifests His eternal beauty through His creatures, His family.

MUSIC

Music is one of the hallmarks of Rumi's teaching. According to him, music is the source of life. To him, music, poetry, and dancing are ways to get closer to God. It was from these ideas he founded the order of the Mawlawi, the "whirling" dervishes, and created the *"sama"*, their sacred dance. *Sama*, according to Rumi, represents a mystical journey of spiritual ascent through mind and love to a state of perfection. The aim is to love and to be of service to the whole of creation, without discrimination against beliefs, races, classes, and nations. The following quotation from Rumi suffices to indicate its place in his teaching:

> All day and night music,
> A quiet, bright reed-song.
> If it fades, we fade.

As we see, there is a direct link between music and life. Furthermore, there is an existential dimension, as well:

> We are as the flute, and the music in us is from You;
> we are as the mountain and the echo in us is from You.

The Mawlawi rites or *sama*, symbolize "the Divine love and mystical ecstasy; they aim at union with the Divine". Music has instrumental meaning together with dance. They are designed to induce a meditative state on the love of God. According to authorities, Mawlawi music contains some of "the most core elements of Eastern classical music" and it serves mainly as an accompaniment for poems of Rumi and other Sufi poets.

The dervishes turn timelessly and effortlessly. They whirl, turning round on their own axis, while moving in an orbit around the room. The right hand is turned up towards heaven to receive God's overflowing mercy that passes through the heart and is transmitted to earth with the left hand turned down. Thus, the whirling dance becomes a bridge between rich and poor.

While one foot remains firmly on the ground, the other crosses it, propelling the dancer around. The rising and falling of the right foot is kept constant by the inner rhythmic repetition of the name of "Allah-Al-lah, Al-lah…[God]" The ceremony can be seen as a great crescendo in three stages:

- Knowing God,
- Seeing God, and
- Uniting with God.

Rumi himself teaches us the meaning of *sama*:

> What is *sama*? A message from the fairy, hidden in your heart;
> with their letter comes serenity to the estranged heart.
> The tree of wisdom comes to bloom with this breeze;
> The inner pores of existence open to this tune.
> When the spiritual cock crows, the dawn arrives;
> When Mars beats his drum victory is ours.
> The essence of the soul was fighting the barrel of the body;
> When it hears the sound of the *daf* [drum] it matures and calms down.
> A wondrous sweetness is sensed in the body;
> It is the sugar that the flute and the flute-player bring to the listener.

In sum, Rumi's teachings present us a rich and meaningful world, which has been created and sustained by God and entrusted to human beings alone. However, we are not the owners and masters of the natural environment, as such. We are only trustees and vicegerents on earth. This stewardship includes the maintenance and utilization of the natural environment in accordance with what God had created these things for, and to take into account the order and the ecological balance of nature on the other.

IV.

Conclusion

Having examined the details of the anthropocentric vision of Confucius and Rumi, I will now try to summarize the similarities and differences between them.

The gist and foundation of Rumi's teaching is a creative transcendental and one God of the Abrahamic tradition. God as creator creates everything from ex-nihilo with creative love. Therefore, love is the source of life. Rumi, therefore, bases his anthropocosmic worldview on the principle of love.

On the other hand, Confucius believes in the creative force of what he calls Heaven or nature. There is no Creator God behind the universe. As a result, Chinese thought is less concerned with theories of origin or with concepts of a personal God than with the perception of an ongoing reality of a self-generating, interconnected universe described by Weiming as a "continuity of being". Therefore, scholars of early Chinese philosophy frequently point to the "organismic, non-transcendent, and non-dualistic conception of the cosmos. However, there is no agreement among scholars what Confucius means by Heaven.

The first similarity between these two great thinkers can be seen when they realized their Divine mission. Confucius said he was fifty when he knew the will of Heaven. The great transformation in Rumi's life began a little earlier, when he was forty years old, but they were both men of later years.

A second similarity concerns the transformative changes in the life of great personalities, which can be called a "rebirth". According to Beck both Confucius with Socrates believed that they had a "mission", and this "Divine-appointed destiny" had a tremendous impact on the rest of their lives. "Because of this relationship with the Divine or a higher power, neither of them seemed to have any fear of death or anything else. Their actions were strictly regulated by their rational or intuitive evaluation of what was right."

Their deaths were similar as well. Confucius died a natural death at the age of seventy-two, while Rumi passed away a natural death at sixty-two, and both accepted death calmly. Rumi declared that "death is [his] wedding with eternity".

It is interesting to find out that both masters based their understanding of nature on an anthropocosmic worldview, which has enormous potential for renewed appreciation of nature as intrinsically valuable, but also as the source of personal vitality and moral integrity for sustaining the community of life.

Moreover, this perspective values nature as the origin of all that sustains life, from the basics of food, clothing, and shelter to innumerable sources of employment. This is, however, not to deny the negative dimensions of the Confucian tradition, nor to claim that historically China was a model of ecological fitness. Rather, it is to suggest ways in which a rethinking of Confucianism may be helpful in our contemporary context. Such a reinterpretation from within the Confucian tradition is already taking place through the efforts of Weiming and other New Confucians.

Where they differ is that Confucius left no book and his legacy has been transmitted through his disciples and tradition. Therefore, when we talk about Confucian values we have to keep in mind the contributions of others. Rumi, however, dictated all of his writings and poems to his disciples himself. We can extract his worldview directly from his writings.

When we study these two thinkers we discover that their ideas about the universe, nature, and human beings are still relevant to the modern world. They can enrich and broaden our perception of nature and ourselves, which, in turn, can establish a basis for ethical awareness of ecological devastation and over-consumption of natural recourses.

More importantly, their wisdom presents and provides us with spiritual resources to overcome, at least, some challenges of our time, and to built bridges of understanding and dialogues among different cultures and civilizations.

REFERENCES

Armstrong, Karen. *The Great Transformation: The Beginning of Our Religious Traditions*, 2006.

Barks, Coleman. *The Essential Rumi*. San Francisco: Harper, 1995.

Bina, Cyrus-Vaziri, Mo. "On the Dialectic of Rumi's Discourse", http://cda.morris.umn.edu/~binac/Essays/RUMI.FINAL.pdf

Chittick, William. *The Sufi Path of Love: the Spiritual Teaching of Rumi*. N.Y.: State University of New York Press, 1983.

Christian Science Monitor, 11/25/97.

Diamond, Jared. *Collapse: How Societies Choose to Fail or Succeed*, Viking Books, 2005.

Geaney, Jane "Chinese Cosmology and Recent Studies in Confucian Ethics", *Journal of Religious Ethics*, Sep 2000, Vol. 28, Issue 3.

Fromm, Erich. *The Art of Loving*, London: George Allen & Unwin Ltd., 1957.

Hardy, Julia M. "Confucianism: The Neglected "Eastern Religion". http://www.muhlenberg.edu/moyer/NEWCONF.html

Huxley, Julian. "Man's Place and Role in Nature" in *New Bottles for New Wine*, New York: Harper & Brothers, 1957.

Iqbal, Afzal. *The Thought of Mohammad Jalal-ud-Din Rumi*. Lahore, Pakistan: Bazm-i Iqbal, 1955.

Jaspers, Karl; Bullock, Michael (Tr.) *The Origin and Goal of History* (1st English ed.). London: Routledge and Keegan Paul, 1953.

Keshavarz, Fatemeh. *Reading Mystical Lyric: The Case of Jalal al-Din Rumi*, University of South Carolina Press, 1998.

Lewis, Franklin D. *Rumi, Past and Present, East and West: the Life, Teachings and Poetry of Jalal al-din Rumi*, Oxford: Oneworld Publications, 2000.

Nasr, Seyyed Hossein, "Islam and Environmental Crisis," in *Spirit and Nature*, ed. Steven C. Rockefeller and John C. Elder, Boston: Beacon Press, 1992.

Needham, Joseph. "Human Laws and Laws of Nature in China and the West (II): Chinese Civilization and the Laws of Nature". *Journal of the History of Ideas*, vol. 12, no. 2, April 1951, pp. 194–230.

Nicholson, Reynold A. *Rumi: Poet and Mystic*, England: Oneworld, 1998.

Özdemir, İbrahim. "Rumi, Jalal al-Din," in *Encyclopedia of Religion and Nature*, ed. Bron Taylor and Jeffrey Kaplan, New York: Continuum, 2003.

Özdemir, İbrahim. "Towards an Understanding of Environmental Ethic from a Qur'anic Perspective", in *Islam and Ecology*, ed. Richard Foltz, Harvard University Press, 2003.

Rolston, III. Holmes "Can the East Help the West to Value Nature?" *Philosophy East and West*, vol. 37, no. 2, *Environmental Ethics,* April 1987, pp. 172–190.

References

Rumi, Jalaluddin. *Discourses of Rumi*, trans: A. J. Arberry, London: John Murray, 1961.

Rumi, Jalaluddin. *Divan-i Kebir*, trans. Nevit O. Ergin, Los Angels: Echo Publicatons, 2000.

Rumi, Jalaluddin. *The Mathnawi of Jalalu'ddin Rumi*. trans. R.A. Nicholson, London: Luzac, 1925–1940.

Sadigh, Soudabeh. "Rumi, Poet of Love and Justice". http://www.payvand.com/news/06/oct/1235.html

Schimmel, Annemarie. *I Am Wind, You Are Fire: the Life and Work of Rumi*. Boston, Mass.: Shambhala Publications, 1992.

Schimmel, Annemarie. *The Triumphal Sun: A Study of the Works of Jalaloddin Rumi*. Albany, N.Y.: State University of New York Press, 1993.

Schimmel, Annemarie. *Look! This Is Love: Poems of Rumi*. Boston, Mass.: Shambhala Publications, 1991.

Smith, Huston. *The Religions of Man*, Harper & Row (New York: 1986).

Star, Jonathan. *Rumi: In the Arms of the Beloved*, New York: Penguin Putnam, 2000.

Tucker, Mary Evelyn -John Berthrong (edts.) "Introduction to Confucianism Confucianism and Ecology: Potential and Limits" in *Confucianism and Ecology*, Harvard/CSWR, 1998.

Weiming, Tu. "The Ecological Turn in New Confucian Humanism: Implications for China and the World" *Daedalus,* Fall 2001.

Whitehead, A. N., *Science and the Modern World*, New York: Macmillan, 1926.

Vitray-Meyerovitch, Eva de. The *Whirling Dervishes: A Commemoration*. London: International Rumi Committee, 1974.

Vitray-Meyerovitch, Eva de. *Rumi and Sufism*, trans: Simone Fattal, Sausalito: The Post-Apollo Press, 1987.

Web sites:
http://en.wikipedia.org/wiki/Confucius
http://www.globalwebpost.com/farooqm/main.htm
http://www.globalwebpost.com/farooqm/study_res/rumi/intro_nicholson.html
http://www.wisdomworld.org/additional/ancientlandmarks/Confucianism.html

APPENDIX I:
Selected Quotations of Confucius

Below are some quotations from the master, which are "full of advice that can be followed easily".

> A man, who has committed a mistake and doesn't correct it, is committing another mistake.

> By three methods we may learn wisdom: First, by reflection, which is noblest; second, by imitation, which is easiest; and third by experience, which is the bitterest.

> He who learns but does not think is lost!
> He who thinks but does not learn is in great danger.

> The essence of knowledge is, having it, to apply it; not having it, to confess your ignorance.

> To see what is right and not to do it, is want of courage.

> I am not one who was born in the possession of knowledge; I am one who is fond of antiquity, and earnest in seeking it there.

To learn and from time to time to apply what one has learnt isn't that a pleasure? ... Learning without thought is labor lost; thought without learning is perilous.

What you do not wish upon yourself, extend not to others.

Everything has its beauty but not everyone sees it.

This equilibrium is the great root from which grow all the human actions in the world, and this harmony is the universal path which they all should pursue.

Study the past, if you would define the future.

Our greatest glory is not in never falling, but in rising every time we fall.

Choose a job you love and you will never have to work a day in your life.

Life is really simple, but we insist on making it complicated.

Every truth has four corners: as a teacher I give you one corner, and it is for you to find the other three.

A journey of a thousand miles begins with a single step.

Before you embark on a journey of revenge, dig two graves.

Everything has its beauty but not everyone sees it.

Forget injuries, never forget kindnesses.

Wherever you go, go with all your heart.

Wheresoever you go, go with all your heart.

Knowing is not as good as loving; loving is not as good as enjoying.

Review the old and deducing the new makes a teacher.

The gentleman understands righteousness, the petty man understands interest.

Aspire to the principle, behave with virtue, abide by benevolence, and immerse yourself in the arts.

Hold faithfulness and sincerity as first principles.

When you have faults, do not fear to abandon them.

A heart set on love will do no wrong.

Sorrow not at being unknown, but seek to be worthy of note.

A father's and a mother's age must be borne in mind; with joy on the one hand, fear on the other.

A gentleman wishes to be slow to speak and quick to act.

Good is no hermit. It has ever neighbors.

There may be men who act without understanding why. I do not. To listen much, pick out the good and follow it; to see much and ponder it: this comes next to understanding.

He does not preach what he practices till he has practiced what he preaches.

He who wishes to secure the good of others has already secured his own.

Real knowledge is to know the extent of one's ignorance.

The superior man acts before he speaks, and afterwards speaks according to his action.

To know that one knows what one knows, and to know that one doesn't know what one doesn't know, there lies true wisdom.

To practice five things under all circumstances constitutes perfect virtue: gravity, generosity of soul, sincerity, earnestness, and kindness.

When you know a thing, to hold that you know it; and when you do not know a thing, to allow that you do not know it—this is knowledge.

He who will not economize will have to agonize.

Old age, believe me, is a good and pleasant thing. It is true you are gently shouldered off the stage, but then you are given such a comfortable front stall as spectator.

APPENDIX II:
Selected Quotations of Rumi

Below are some quotation from the wisdom and wit of Jalaluddin Rumi which are full of love and life. If translated into action, as Rumi advise us, they can enrich and change our life.

> He is a letter to everyone. You open it. It says, 'Live!'

> The rain is weeping and the sun is burning twine together to make us grow. Keep your intelligence white-hot and your grief glistening, so your life will stay fresh. Cry easily like a little child.

> Let's ask God to help us to self-control for one who lacks it, lacks his grace.

> The intelligent want self-control; children want candy.

> The lion who breaks the enemy's ranks is a minor hero compared to the lion who overcomes himself.

Since in order to speak, one must first listen, learn to speak by listening.

When your heart becomes the grave of your secrets, that desire of yours will be gained more quickly. The prophet said that anyone who keeps secret his inmost thought will soon attain the object of his desire. When seeds are buried in the earth, their inward secrets become the flourishing garden.

The sword of reality is the saint's protection.

Patience is the key to joy.

Fasting is the first principle of medicine.

I am burning. If anyone lacks tinder, let him set his rubbish ablaze with my fire.

My friend, the Sufi is the friend of the present moment. To say "tomorrow" is not our way.

On the way there is no harder pass than this: fortunate is he who does not carry envy as his companion.

Stay with friends who support you in these. Talk with them about sacred texts, and how you are doing, and how they are doing, and keep your practices together.

Brother stand the pain
Escape the poison of your impulses.
The sky will bow to your beauty, if you do.
Learn to light the candle. Rise with the sun.

Turn away from the cave of your sleeping.
That way a thorn expands to a rose.
A particular glows with the universal."
"Little by little, wean yourself.
This is the gist of what I have to say.
From an embryo whose nourishment comes in the blood,
move to an infant drinking milk,
to a child on solid food,
to a searcher after wisdom,
to a hunter of invisible game.

Know that a word suddenly shot from the tongue is like an arrow shot from the bow. Son, that arrow won't turn back on its way; you must damn the torrent at its source.

Everything in the universe is a pitcher brimming with wisdom and beauty.

If you are irritated by every rub, how will you be polished?

Burdens are the foundations of ease and bitter things the forerunners of pleasure.

O, happy the soul that saw its own faults.

Students of cunning have consumed their hearts and learned only tricks; they've thrown away real riches: patience, self-sacrifice, generosity. Rich though opens the way.

The beginning of pride and hatred lies in worldly desire, and the strength of your desire if from habit. When an evil tendency becomes confirmed by habit, rage is triggered when anyone restrains you.

Conventional opinion is the ruin of our souls.

No mirror ever became iron again;
No bread ever became wheat;
No ripened grape ever became sour fruit.
Mature yourself and be secure from a change for the worse.
Become the light.

People of the world don't look at themselves, and so they blame one another.

You think the shadow is the substance.

Travelers, it is late. Life's sun is going to set. During these brief days that you have strength, be quick and spare no effort of your wings.

That which is false troubles the heart, but truth brings joyous tranquility.
The middle path is the way to wisdom.
Be occupied, then, with what you really value and let the thief take something else.
God turns you from one feeling to another and teaches by means of opposites, so that you will have two wings to fly, not one.

Beware! Don't allow yourself to do what you
know is wrong, relying on the thought, 'Later
I will repent and ask God's forgiveness.'

Pale sunlight,
pale the wall.
Love moves away.
The light changes
I need more grace
than I thought.

I am neither Christian nor Jew,
nor Magian, nor Muslim.
I am not of the East, nor the West,
not of the land, nor the sea.
I am not from nature's mine,
nor from the circling stars.
I am neither of earth nor water,
neither of wind nor fire.
I am not of the empyrean,
nor of the dust on this carpet.
I am not of the deep, nor from behind.
I am not of India or China,
not of Bulgaria, nor Saqsin;
I am not of the kingdom of Iraqain,
nor of the land of Khorasan.
I am not of this world nor the next,
not of heaven, nor of purgatory.
My place is the placeless,
my trace is the traceless.
It is not the body nor is it the soul,
for I belong to the soul of my love.

I have put duality away
and seen the two worlds as one.
One I seek, One I know.
One I see, One I call.
He is the First, He is the Last.
He is the outward, He is the Inward.
I know of nothing but *Hu* (He), none but him.
Intoxicated with the cup of love,
two worlds slip from my hands.

ABOUT THE AUTHOR

Prof. Dr. İbrahim Özdemir is the rector of Gazikent University, in Gaziantep, Turkey. He has traveled widely in the Muslim world and the West. Özdemir addresses a variety of audiences on topics related to the philosophy of religion, world religions, Sufism, environmental philosophy, sustainable development, religion and the environment, interfaith dialogue, and Islamic studies.

For more information:

http://www.ibrahimozdemir.com

iozdemir@yahoo.com